A Courteous Approach to Qur'an

-Insights from Selected Talks-

Shaykh Fadhlalla Haeri

Zahra Publications

Zahra Publications

The author would like to thank all volunteers who helped to bring this booklet to production.

Published by Zahra Publications
www.shaykhfadhlallahaeri.com
www.zahrapublications.pub

Designed and typeset in South Africa by Quintessence Publishing

Set in 11 point on 15 point, Garamond
Printed and bound by Lightning Source

ISBN (Printed Version) - Paperback: 978-1-9-28329-47-3

TABLE OF CONTENTS

PUBLISHER'S NOTE

The invocation of 'Peace be upon Him' is implied at every mention of the Prophet Muhammad and Prophet Ibrahim.

Any reference to 'men' in the text has the connotation of humankind and equally refers to women and should be regarded as non-gender specific.

INTRODUCTION

The Qur'an addresses most issues that concern human beings with constant references to the ultimate Reality and Truth. Considerable emphasis is given to relative time and human concerns on earth and the connection between the inseparability of the relative and the Absolute. The Qur'an emphasises that anything that exists or happens is due to God and equally emphasises human responsibility to act and live with clear accountability to God.

The main difference between other traditions and religions at the time of the Prophet Muhammad is the perplexing notion that, in truth, there is only God, and all else are shadows in this Light. This most potent thread of God's perpetual presence and dominance is considered the higher path of Muhammad towards an awakening to absolute Truth, without denying the relative and transient realities.

The mind is the connector between the infinite unseen and the relative earthly dualities. The heart is considered the seat of the soul or the spirit and the connecting point to the light of life itself. The duality of human nature is such that it seamlessly connects the so-called individual, whose personal life begins with birth and ends with death to perpetual life itself.

The essential message of the Qur'an has two beams: one which illuminates the fundamental nature of absolute Oneness and the other beam which is the acceptance, realisation and living of this information as the purpose of this life, to be fully revealed in the Hereafter. If one has not awakened to the Truth in this life, it will be apparent in the hereafter without the shadows of egos and other distractions. The individual's soul or spirit within the heart intrinsically knows this truth and transmits it to the living person at a higher level of consciousness. This awareness brings about lasting fulfilment when followed or misery, fear and sickness if ignored. The idea of heaven and hell after death emphasises the natural outcome of human intention and action in this life.

To understand the Qur'an and use it as a template, this brief background is necessary. This booklet presents extracts from talks I have given on the subject, arranged in six themes: Context and Action, the Self, Understanding, Transformation, Awakening and lastly Oneness and Balance.

Shaykh Fadhlalla Haeri

1. CONTEXT & ACTION
1.1 Historical Context: A Culture of Generosity

To gain blessings and mercy from this ultimate, balanced book of wisdom, you must put it into the right perspective. This means you must appreciate the historical context, i.e., the overall condition of genuine Bedouins and nomads at that time.

They constantly confronted their physical demise, yet generosity was their highest value and most honoured characteristic. When one is close to starvation, generosity is the most meritorious of actions.

They were a people of self-reliance, dependent on their reading of the situation around them, of nature and, ultimately, Allah. Their strength came through this self-reliance, self-respect and consistent belief in a favourable outcome.

One of the critical approaches to the Qur'an should therefore include understanding the situation in Makkah and Madinah during the time of its revelation.

Identify the historical period under which the chapter or verse was revealed to understand and place it in perspective.

1.2 Migration (*Hijrah*) of Correct Action

Despite the afflictions faced by the Prophet Muhammad during the Makkan period, he expressed contentment and was a fountain of blessings. His actions were consistently compassionate, understanding, wise, patient and persevering. He worked for the sake of Allah, for nature and the evolution and revolution of the heart. The 11th, 12th and 13th year of his prophet-hood in Makkah spelt the polarisation of the new way of life with the old tribal habits. The people of Makkah saw the Prophet Muhammad as one of their sons threatening their traditional values. He criticised ancient customs, e.g. the dishonour of fathering a daughter—ironic when a father himself is born of a woman.

People were also troubled by the message that this indescribable, intangible entity is behind all you witness—an entity to which you can only allude, understandable only through the throne of the heart. The codification of this new system became a real threat, and a clash was inevitable.

The Prophet Muhammad's perspective was to see those thirteen years of affliction as years of blessedness. All reflective human beings will retrospectively look at their formative years and realise the sweetness and simplicity of past troubles.

Those who trust the perfection of the *Ahl al-Bayt* (Members of the Prophet's household) and their Schools of Teaching have the advantage of seeing the lives of their Imams as a perfect reflection of the spirit of the Prophet Muhammad and source of guidance for correct conduct.

We see the same *ruh* (soul) and values lived over a period of about three hundred years and can derive many lessons from them. One's own imam, guide, or teacher, should reflect the same spirit of compassion, generosity, understanding, and wisdom as the Prophet Muhammad.

Seek the meanings of the verses and their explanation since the Qur'an encompasses the expounding of everything. This is so that the deep connotations may be exposed to the seeker. Allah bestows upon man an understanding of His book. The Qur'an constantly repeats phrases such as 'Will you then not consider?'

2. THE SELF
2.1 Connecting Surah (Chapter) with Self

The Qur'an is for all people across all times; thus, the reader must internalise its guidance. Realise that the guidance offered is prescriptive rather than superstitious. A human being is constantly confronted by the conflict of opposites and must learn to deal with these dualities—in a manner appropriate to each situation.

The Qur'an displays through every chapter its *sūh* (fortress of high walls) so that as one delves deeper, one enters that safe harbour. Every chapter is also a stepping stone that you have taken for yourself, and if it leaves an imprint in your heart, then the chapter (or verse) and your heart have connected.

Allah says:

تَبْصِرَةً وَذِكْرَىٰ لِكُلِّ عَبْدٍ مُّنِيبٍ ۝

Giving insight and a reminder for every servant who turns [to Allah]. (50:8)

Knowledge and understanding of one's state, its opposing factors and weaknesses, are essential for the chapter to connect to the self.

Do not have any sense of power or ability; do not look upon yourself with eyes of satisfaction. Seek forgiveness from Allah and be grateful. Abandon yourself in true submission and do not judge yourself as good or bad.

2.2 Being Human

Humans have travelled to higher atmospheres yet we hardly know anything about our inner space. Inside our humanness, the Qur'an reminds us that we are a *nafs* (spirit and ego).

$$وَنَفْسٍ وَمَا سَوَّىٰهَا ۝ فَأَلْهَمَهَا فُجُورَهَا وَتَقْوَىٰهَا ۝$$

And [by] the soul and He who proportioned it. And inspired it [with discernment of] its wickedness and its righteousness.
(91:7-8)

Nafs is the same word as *nafas*, which means 'breathing'. We depend wholly on breath (air), water, earth and fire. Without these four essential elements, we cannot survive. The above verses urge us to look at the self and how it has been designed to fluctuate between its decadence and needs.

We are distracted by all the fires around us, in our business, work, with other human beings, with the debt we have created, with our families.

There is no time left for us to smell the Garden that is beckoning us. These distractions ultimately overwhelm our being and divert us from our true intention and purpose to focus on the Garden and enter it. Every self, every human being, knows what they are doing. We want status, we want wealth, we want to be admired, and we want to be be loved. We know what we are doing, yet we give excuses.

بَلْ تُؤْثِرُونَ ٱلْحَيَوٰةَ ٱلدُّنْيَا ۝ وَٱلْأَخِرَةُ خَيْرٌ وَأَبْقَىٰ ۝

But you prefer the worldly life. While the Hereafter is better and everlasting. (87:16-17)

The Prophet put his hand around Salman al-Farsi and told him that *Jannah* (Paradise) needs and is waiting for him. The awakened being in this world travels with ease and equanimity towards the natural destiny of consciousness of the hereafter.

We are limited, having emerged from the limitless and eventually returning to infinity. Infinity begins every instant. Every moment is the beginning of a new infinity, but we are oblivious. We cannot move on if we cannot stop the mind from constantly going to the past and being insecure about the future. Memories and emotions are barriers to the present and taint our faith in the future. That is why our *salāh* (prayer) is conditional upon *hudūr ul-qalb* (presence of heart). Our hearts must be tranquil and present, and then we disappear. The Qur'an says about *insān* (man):

$$ وَكُلَّ إِنسَٰنٍ أَلْزَمْنَٰهُ طَٰٓئِرَهُۥ فِى عُنُقِهِۦ ﴾ $$

And [for] every person We have imposed his fate upon his neck
(17:13)

Whatever we do, our actions are upon us. We must be responsible regarding our thoughts, intentions and actions because we will witness the consequences clearly after death. For this reason, the Prophet Muhammad says, 'He who has died, his *Qiyāmah* (Reckoning) has happened'. This is because we can no longer act. We can, however, rectify past actions by seeking forgiveness or being available to help and serve those less fortunate than ourselves.

Constant awareness of death will bring about modesty and *zuhud* (renouncing of worldly pleasures) as we are all *arwāh* (souls) as described above (17:13). In the *Akhirah* (Hereafter) every self is driven by that inner force of the *rūh* (soul) and the witnessing upon us of what we have done and thought.

وَجَآءَتْ كُلُّ نَفْسٍ مَّعَهَا سَآئِقٌ وَشَهِيدٌ ۝

And every soul will come, with it a driver and a witness. (50:21)

Every cell declares it. As the Qur'an says:

بَلِ ٱلْإِنسَـٰنُ عَلَىٰ نَفْسِهِۦ بَصِيرَةٌ ۝

Rather, man, against himself, will be a witness (75:14)

19

Rise to a state where you hear Allah's words directly from the Speaker and not from yourself. To clear your mind, free your body and rūh (soul) and to ultimately progress and rise from lower to higher consciousness, resume your approach to the Qur'an.

2.3 The Complete Human Being

Completion relates to understanding our conditioned and relative consciousness with constant reference to soul consciousness and its boundlessness. Completion implies full awareness of humanity and Divinity being, seamlessly connected. This potential is in every one of us. We call the Prophet Muhammad an *Insān al-Kāmil* (a complete/perfect human being). This does not mean that he had a perfect body or perfect sight. These are all decaying. He was the perfect being in that he was resonating with the perfect light of Allah. He was the *nur* (light) of Allah in human form. That is why we love to see human beings resonate with humanity and Divinity, for every one of us is both.

We have the *Nūr* of *ar-Rahmān* (the Merciful) in our hearts, and we have the shadows and dreadfulness of *Shaytān* (the rejected one). The more you attune yourself to *ar-Rahmān*, the more *Shaytān* will be subdued. It is present, but you are unafflicted by it, i.e. not listening to its *waswās* (whisperings). That is the purpose of completing our responsibility, duty and delights in this life.

This life can be a delightful journey if you take reference from and calibrate yourself with your *rūh* (soul). It becomes a misery and a battlefield if your desires are powered by your *nafs* (ego) and you constantly try to please others. Do not confuse this with your attempt to be helpful and kind. This should continue with the realisation that you will never be able to please anyone, least of all yourself. Thus, you should do what you can and ask Allah's forgiveness. Declare your limitations and dedicate your intention and attention to that which matters most.

If you know this infinite *rūh* (soul) in you, then you are on the path of Divine knowledge, a truly spiritual path. When you follow only rituals and literalism, your path loses its vitality to revive, rejuvenate and guide you towards arrival. We need rituals, outer restrictions and boundaries to discover the boundless. We accept boundaries and limitations to know in our hearts that He, Who is beyond boundaries and limits, will inspire and guide us because one of His names is *al-Hadi* (the Guide).

Feel the Qur'an. Flow with every verse in accordance with your surrender to it. A person is affected and becomes characterised by the quality of the verses recited. Take of the Qur'an as little or as much will suffice for you, according to your ability and state.

فَٱقْرَءُوا۟ مَا تَيَسَّرَ مِنَ ٱلْقُرْءَانِ

Read of it what is made easy for you (73:20)

2.4 True Meaning of *'Adab'* (Appropriate Courtesy)

The person who is utterly courteous towards his or herself is likely to be courteous towards their Creator. Once this courtesy is present, spontaneous behaviour can be refined, i.e. the ability to tune in the ability to tune in to the present and benefit from the foolishness of others instead of suffering from it.

Torment is the first part of good fortune, and without this torment, i.e. *nafs al-ammārah* (subjugated by the *nafs*/lower self), you are barred from your inner connectedness. Accordingly, the meaning of behaviour under different circumstances, the understanding and implication of courage, steadfastness and ultimately, the significance of belief in Allah, are all translated into action.

إِنَّ رَبَّكَ هُوَ يَفْصِلُ بَيْنَهُمْ يَوْمَ ٱلْقِيَـٰمَةِ فِيمَا كَانُوا۟ فِيهِ يَخْتَلِفُونَ ۝

Indeed, your Lord will judge between them on the Day of Resurrection concerning that over which they used to differ.
(32:25)

23

There may be certain things that come to the heart when reading certain verses, and that is sufficient— if it is of value to you. *Adab* (appropriate courtesy) and its applicability to us require understanding the us require understanding the content without separating it from its context.

Imam Ali said: 'There is no good in an act of worship which is not understood by its doer nor in the Qur'an reading which is not understood and acted upon.' The purpose of reading the Qur'an is to reflect upon its meaning. Read more than one tafsir (commentary), allowing the Qur'an to have its effect upon you by pondering over the meanings.

3. UNDERSTANDING
3.1 Building Blocks for Understanding

'Alif Lām Mēm'. Letters are the first steps or building blocks, which are the foundation of a sentence. The secret of the letters is based on the mystery of creation, on the amazing secret of communication. *'Alif Lām Mēm'* is a matter of conjecture, i.e. it is subject to in-depth interpretation. Commentators say they are the firm signs. Understanding is thus relative. Sometimes, you may understand, and sometimes you may not.

All care, governance, patterns and organisations in every living system, ecologically or otherwise, stem from the Source. The metaphor of the power of the Source of all light is radiantly reflected in the following significant verse:

اَللَّهُ نُورُ ٱلسَّمَٰوَٰتِ وَٱلْأَرْضِ

Allah is the Light of the heavens and earth (24:35)

Allah has sent the Book containing all the manifestations of His creation, and the Qur'an is *muhkam* (can be translated based on wisdom).

An example of this is a verse of the Qur'an:

$$إِلَى رَبِّهَا نَاظِرَةٌ ﴿٢٣﴾$$

To their Lord they look. (75:23)

Some say this verse is *mutashābih* (allegorical/metaphorical meaning) because we know Allah cannot be seen. He sees all and is the cause of your sight. The blocks you require to build your understanding will become apparent with time. Where the signs of the Qur'an appear to be confusing or unclear, it is only because of one's lack of clarity. The signs are *maknūn* (hidden or concealed) in the *Qur'an al Mubīn* (clear or evident Qur'an). There appear to be many human beings, yet only one humanity exists. Time and experience delude us into beliefs of understanding with thoughts such as, 'I am wiser now'. Be wary of falling into the trap of ignorance and arrogance. Recognise that the sea of knowledge is unending in yourself and your building blocks.

Do not read the Qur'an in isolation. Use the Qur'an as a manual and let the reflection be seen and felt in your heart.

3.2 Reflective Understanding of the Path of Islam

The path of Islam is based on the Qur'an, which is the Divine half (acknowledgement of the Oneness of God), with the other half being the *Sunnah* (Customary practice, line of conduct used in reference to Allah or the prophet Muhammad), and Muhammadi application of it. One can find the answer to everything that matters within these two halves.

To truly know the meaning of this path, you must be willing to live by it and apply it. Unless you do this, it will have little or no meaning. To accomplish this, there must be trust in an accessible human form, such as the Prophet Muhammad. Every heart seeks to trust and see goodness in everything. Thus, those who believed in the Prophet Muhammad began to have a true belief and trust in Allah.

Inner and outer courtesy must be applied when attempting to learn from the Qur'an. This enables you to absorb it and how it came to its specific values, meanings, explanations and application by the Prophet Muhammad, his *Ahl al-Bayt* (Members of the Prophet's household) and worthy *Sahābah* (Companions of the Prophet). Without the interpretations by the Prophet Muhammad and his household, we would be at a loss.

وَلْيَخْشَ ٱلَّذِينَ لَوْ تَرَكُواْ مِنْ خَلْفِهِمْ ذُرِّيَّةً ضِعَٰفًا خَافُواْ عَلَيْهِمْ فَلْيَتَّقُواْ ٱللَّهَ وَلْيَقُولُواْ قَوْلًا سَدِيدًا ۝

And let those [executors and guardians] fear [injustice] as if they [themselves] had left weak offspring behind and feared for them. So, let them fear Allah and speak words of appropriate justice. (4:9)

Discriminate sufficiently to recognise right from wrong. Return to the everlasting truthfulness of the Source.

3.3 The Heart as a Faculty of Understanding

We have an inner sense of *mutafakkira* (contemplation), which receives an impression, sends it to the heart (not the mind) and gets an answer. The *yatafakkarūn* (those who reflect and contemplate) are often mentioned in the Qur'an.

You need a living heart but must use your mind to receive signals from the heart. The ability to catch yourself and prevent yourself from acting on impulse and the ability to monitor your actions are by-products of a healthy heart and have nothing to do with the mind. The mind is only for rationality and acts as a memory box or hard-drive.

In the verses below, the Qur'an presents lessons from history where Pharaoh exercised his powers of manipulation and over-calculation, which proved fatal for him.

إِنَّهُ فَكَّرَ وَقَدَّرَ ۝ فَقُتِلَ كَيْفَ قَدَّرَ ۝

He thought and plotted [against the Qur'an]. So, let him be cursed: how he plotted [against the Truth]. (74:18-19)

The lesson is for the reader to be wary of the mind taking the lead. Thus, a strong mind can also be the worst obstacle for us. A sound mind and a free, open, healthy heart, distinguishing between actual signals and whims, are vital.

Nothing should stand between you and your Creator. No Imam, spiritual leader or even your faith should act as a filter between you and the Qur'an. If the reader realises this, he will read it just as the slave reads the writing of his master to him, that he may think and reflect upon it and then act accordingly.

3.4 Turning to the *Nur* (light) of the Heart

فَأَمَّا ٱلَّذِينَ فِى قُلُوبِهِمْ زَيْغٌ

As for those in whose hearts is deviation [from Truth] (3:7)

The root of *zaygh* (above verse) is *zaghā*, which means "to deviate or swerve or turn aside". We have come from Allah, are sustained by His grace and are returning to everlasting Truthfulness. Thus, we realise that, ultimately, there is no deviation or turning away. The one who turns away has a distracted heart.

Our hearts deviate or meander when they are not connected with Reality and are not in complete trust in the mercy of Allah under all circumstances. *Nur* (light) is in the heart. The light of the Source of all creation is a light within your heart, i.e. already within you. This internal light is everlasting but veiled. Be wary of the faltering and drifting heart, which follows its whims and is easily distracted by glitter. Remove the veils between your self, your heart and your Creator.

Those who study the Qur'an from the outside receive nothing from it. Turn away from the *fitnah* (mischief or charm), which is only a plot to distract you.

$$\text{وَلَقَدْ نَجَّيْنَا بَنِيٓ إِسْرَٰٓءِيلَ مِنَ ٱلْعَذَابِ ٱلْمُهِينِ ﴿٣٠﴾}$$

And We certainly saved the Children of Israel from the humiliating torment. (44:30)

Persons of knowledge know in their hearts that there is only Allah. Thus, the irreconcilable common occurrence of two Muslims fighting each other means that either neither of them is in Islam, or one is not. A person who has submitted to Allah is the hand of Allah, and the Grace of Allah sustains him.

*Learn the Arabic in the Qur'an by the Qur'an.
Endeavour to find the root meaning of the text and ponder
over the connection between their various derivations. This
will enhance your understanding and provide you with
clarity. Further, learn what is necessary and valuable of
the Qur'an's outward explanation that has come to us from
the best Source.*

3.5 The Beautiful Affliction of Knowledge

True knowledge is possessed by those who know the
root or the real, deep meaning. Thus, it is incumbent
on us to seek helpers with the knowledge and the
ability to give light to the inner self. When you are
afflicted with that beautiful affliction of knowledge
and wisdom, you know when to act or not and
avoid planting seeds in barren ground. This state
of presence brings about a constant awareness, i.e.
alertness and being fully alive.

طَاعَةٌ وَقَوْلٌ مَّعْرُوفٌ فَإِذَا عَزَمَ ٱلْأَمْرُ فَلَوْ صَدَقُوا۟ ٱللَّهَ
لَكَانَ خَيْرًا لَّهُمْ ۞

Obedience and good words. And when the matter [of fighting] was determined, if they had been true to Allah, it would have been better for them. (47:21)

An essential approach to the Qur'an is to begin knowing oneself first. Remember that true knowledge comes from unveiling. If not, knowledge itself is a veil between man and Lord.

4. TRANSFORMATION
4.1 Conditions for Transformation through the Qur'an.

The Qur'an is an interactive manual for wholesome living for individuals and the collective. It describes the emergence of the universe and all diverse dualities from a cosmic Unity, which is also its ultimate destiny. It also describes pathways that enhance higher consciousness, lessening human suffering and fears.

The ultimate gift in life is to be awakened to the truth that all perceptions of space and time are temporary states emanating from cosmic perpetual Unity.

Our limited freedom is to learn the boundaries and how to relate to creation. This allows us to be finely attuned to the Source of life, thereby overcoming the fear of death.

The way of the Qur'an is to show you a means of transcendence from limitations. By stopping the mind, which confirms these limitations, you can transcend. Be prepared to get out of the confinement of space and time.

The most critical approach to the Qur'an is being humble and bereft, knowing that you are approaching the ultimate. The method is to lose the self and let the soul unite with its origin—to go beyond stillness into another zone of consciousness.

- *Fu'ad* (The Inner heart that never lies/remains firm)

The Qur'an covers all people across time. We can either believe in it, and its message will be revealed to us, or we can attempt to question it and receive no benefit from it. Allah is not there to be questioned. Have courtesy with the knowledge that we have come from nowhere. Once reasoning has been exhausted and we have been extinguished through passion, *fu'ad* is gained. Limited energy must be preserved from 'outer in-vestment' for 'inner in-vestment', without sacrificing worldly responsibilities and the need for appropriate action. Allah has created us in this world for the other world. We have been created for both. If we deny one, we will be denied the other.

- *Amal* (Action)

Amal is to internalise and manifest what is inside you to externalise an intention. We all want to be among those who believe and do righteous deeds, as referred to in numerous verses in the Qur'an. It is both a response and impulse, emerging from one's *fitrah* (true nature) cracking open. We are trying to unite our outer world with our inner world.

- Uniting the inner and outer

We outwardly experience the world, which has its *adab* (appropriate courtesy) and its map; it requires the use of the intellect to its utmost ability. However, the world of the unseen needs an entirely different logic. As described earlier, it requires coming to the Qur'an with humility and purity of heart, acknowledging your ignorance. The approach to the unseen and the Hereafter is to be dead—to cease to exist. All prophetic practices in all religions and all authentic teachings show us this dichotomy. Our confusion often precludes us from seeing this dichotomy with clarity.

There are, therefore, two different domains, as in Chapter *ar-Rahmān* below:

$$بَيْنَهُمَا بَرْزَخٌ لَّا يَبْغِيَانِ ۝$$

Between them is a barrier [so] neither of them transgresses.
(55:20)

Only the *rūh* (soul) and the heart of the human being encompass inner and outer consciousness, i.e. the world outside and the infinite unseen world (beyond time and space). This is one of the meanings of the verse that an *amānah* (trust) was given:

$$لَوْ أَنزَلْنَا هَٰذَا الْقُرْءَانَ عَلَىٰ جَبَلٍ لَّرَأَيْتَهُ خَٰشِعًا مُّتَصَدِّعًا مِّنْ خَشْيَةِ اللَّهِ ۚ وَتِلْكَ الْأَمْثَٰلُ نَضْرِبُهَا لِلنَّاسِ لَعَلَّهُمْ يَتَفَكَّرُونَ ۝$$

If We had sent down this Qur'an upon a mountain, you would have seen it humbled and coming apart from fear of Allah. And these examples We present to the people that perhaps they will give thought. (59:21)

The mountains are within earthly dualities and their natural laws, whereas the Qur'an contains beams of the Absolute beyond all dualities. Praise be to Allah,

Who has given us access to Him through His Prophet Muhammad and His Book, which was revealed as described:

$$في كِتَٰبٍ مَّكْنُونٍ ۝۷۸$$

$$لَّا يَمَسُّهُۥٓ إِلَّا ٱلْمُطَهَّرُونَ ۝۷۹ تَنزِيلٌ مِّن رَّبِّ ٱلْعَٰلَمِينَ ۝۸۰$$

In a register, well-protected. Which none may touch except those who are purified. A revelation from the Lord of the worlds.
(56:78-80)

At the human level, we are thinking animals with an intellect that takes us to the edge of the unknown. The Qur'an's message, 'Light upon light' (24:35), is to show how humanity and Divinity are inseparable. Shadows and dualities are attributes of the human plane of existence, whereas cosmic perfection and total awareness are from the zone of Essence and Light. To read the Qur'an is to know the absolute Truth, which manifests as countless relative realities and shadows of the human mind and intellect, without denying the relativity of dualities.

You must apply your mind and heart to enter the ocean of light and delight. As Imam Hassan said,

'Act accordingly; for Allah gives to him, who acts according to that which he knows, the knowledge of that which he did not know'. He also said, 'Those before you regarded the Qur'an as a message from their Lord. They used to contemplate on it by night and live by it by day'. Here, reference is made to direct Qur'anic injunctions and prohibitions and to every single verse contained within.

وَٱلَّذِينَ جَٰهَدُواْ فِينَا لَنَهْدِيَنَّهُمْ سُبُلَنَا ۚ وَإِنَّ ٱللَّهَ لَمَعَ ٱلْمُحْسِنِينَ ﴿٦٩﴾

And those who strive for Us—We will surely guide them to Our ways. And indeed, Allah is with the doers of good. (29:69)

Humans have always wondered about their origin and destination. People of different nations and backgrounds referred to numerous scriptures and sacred texts. The Islamic Muhammadi message, which has been modified and adapted over centuries from the Abrahamic tradition, emphasises the essential Oneness of the universe and its perfect governance by the ever-present Divine Source.

وَلَقَدْ أَنزَلْنَآ إِلَيْكُمْ ءَايَتٍ مُّبَيِّنَتٍ وَمَثَلًا مِّنَ ٱلَّذِينَ
خَلَوۡاْ مِن قَبۡلِكُمۡ وَمَوۡعِظَةً لِّلۡمُتَّقِينَ ﴿٣٤﴾

And We have certainly sent down to you, distinct verses and
examples from those who passed on before you and an admonition
for those who fear Allah. (24:34)

The highest and noblest science of the Qur'an is
the knowledge of Allah, i.e. the knowledge for
which it is intended. All other forms of knowledge
are sought for the sake of this higher knowledge.
When one attains knowledge of Allah (*ar-Rabb*; the
Sustainer), one attains knowledge of one's self. As
the Prophet Muhammad said, 'Whoever knows his
self, knows his Sustainer.'

4.2 Outer Approaches for Transformation through the Qur'an

• Be in a state of *wudu* (ritual ablution).

• Sit or stand facing *qiblah* (direction Muslims face
  when praying, towards the *Ka'ba* in Mecca) if
  possible.

- Display a respectful attitude as if in the presence of your teacher.
- Seek refuge in Allah from *Shaytān*.

$$فَإِذَا قَرَأْتَ ٱلْقُرْءَانَ فَٱسْتَعِذْ بِٱللَّهِ مِنَ ٱلشَّيْطَٰنِ ٱلرَّجِيمِ ۝$$

So, when you recite the Qur'an, seek refuge with Allah from the accursed Shaytān. (16:98)

- Calm yourself inwardly and outwardly, ensuring that your energy, focus and efforts align with your intention.
- Ask from Allah before, during and after reciting the Qur'an.
- Use a clear and beautiful script to read from.
- Be consistent in reciting the Qur'an. If you find it helpful, divide your reading into several parts to progressively move through the entire book.
- It is essential to remember your Creator at all times. Thus, a Qur'anic recital is appropriate at any time. After all, how can the One Who has given you memory be forgotten?
- Assume that each recitation is the last you will hear before you die. It is not about the amount recited but rather the quality of transformation.

- Read slowly and distinctly, alone or in a group.
- 'Adorn the Qur'an with your voices', said the Prophet Muhammad. This will move your heart and those who may hear you. As Allah says,

$$وَرَتِّلِ ٱلْقُرْءَانَ تَرْتِيلًا$$

And recite the Qur'an in slow, measured rhythmic tones. (73:4)

- Recite the Qur'an and reflect on its meaning.
- If you cannot recite the Qur'an in Arabic, read the Book in your language or listen to a recital of the verses you intend to read. Listen to and perceive the melodious sound of a Qur'an reciter which resonates with you. If you can, by the second or third hearing, try to follow and recite along with the text.
- Make *sajdah* (prostration) when listening to or reciting any of the fourteen verses in the Qur'an where a *sajdah* is called for. During such a *sajdah*, appreciate that you are prostrating before the mighty Creator, Who has given you countless blessings.
- Pay attention and practice constant presence— know where and why you are there. Open up

and let your heart take the lead; free your mind from present clutter and past baggage; abandon whisperings from your lower self; switch off external senses; and turn away from all else and realign your inner self to Allah.

- Do not let idle thoughts, obsessions or habits hinder your understanding. Once you have successfully emptied your mind, allow the purity of the Qur'an to flow into you.

4.3 Inner Approaches for Transformation through the Qur'an

- Identify the historical period in which the chapter or verse was revealed to understand and place it in perspective.
- Seek the meanings of the verses and their explanations, since the Qur'an encompasses the exposition of everything. This is so that the deep connotations may be exposed to the seeker. Allah bestows upon humanity an understanding of His book. The Qur'an constantly repeats phrases such as 'Will you then not consider?'
- Do not read the Qur'an in isolation. Use the

Qur'an as a manual and let the reflection be seen and felt in your heart.

- Discriminate sufficiently to recognise right from wrong. Return to the everlasting truthfulness of the Source.

- Nothing should stand between you and your Creator. No imam, spiritual leader or even your faith, should act as a filter between you and the Qur'an. If the reader realises this, he will read it just as the servant reads the writing of his master to him, that he may think and reflect upon it and then act accordingly.

- An essential approach to the Qur'an is to begin knowing oneself first. Remember that true knowledge comes from unveiling. If not, knowledge itself is a veil between man and Lord.

- Do not have any sense of power or ability; do not look upon yourself with eyes of satisfaction. Seek forgiveness from Allah and be grateful. Abandon yourself in genuine submission, and do not judge yourself as either good or bad.

- Rise to a state wherein you hear Allah's words directly from the Speaker and not from yourself. To clear your mind, free your body and *rūh* (soul)

45

and ultimately progress and rise from lower to higher consciousness, resume your approach to the Qur'an.

- Feel the Qur'an. Flow with every verse in accordance with your surrender to it. Take from the Qur'an as little or as much will suffice for you, according to your ability and state.

$$فَٱقْرَءُوا۟ مَا تَيَسَّرَ مِنَ ٱلْقُرْءَانِ$$

Read of it what is made easy for you (73:20)

- Imam Ali said: 'There is no good in an act of worship which is not understood by its doer, nor in the reading of Qur'an which is not understood and acted upon.' The purpose of reading the Qur'an is to reflect on its meaning. Read more than one *tafsir* (commentary), allowing the Qur'an to have its effect upon you by pondering over the meanings.

- Do not be content with or stop at mere outward explanations of the Qur'an. As the Qur'an repeats phrases, so too should you repeat and find reflective explanations. Read recommended commentaries and give yourself time to reflect upon what you have understood. Dive in with conscientiousness and encompass yourself with the knowledge of the Qur'an.

- Allah is the One Creator of space and time. Thus, read and contemplate what you read, knowing the message is timeless and self-empowering.

- To be kind and just to yourself—read, recite, listen, resonate, and calibrate.

- Connect the exaltedness of Divine speech to the glory of Its Speaker by reflecting upon His Attributes, Majesty and Works in creation. Understand Allah's kindness towards His creatures through revelation in letters and sounds suitable for men's attributes and intellects. Know that what you read is for you to digest.

- Know that every verse is a verse for you. From each verse will be derived that which its reader needs. This points towards the pure awareness and remembrance referred to in the Qur'an by the word *dhikr* (remembrance).

5. AWAKENING

5.1 Awakening to the Truth

Your approach to the Qur'an must steer your heart and mind to the path of transformation. The Prophet Muhammad continuously recited the following *du'a* (prayer):

$$اَللّٰهُمَّ أَرِنَا الْحَقَّ حَقًّا وَّارْزُقْنَا اتِّبَاعَه، وَأَرِنَا الْبَاطِلَ بَاطِلًا وَّارْزُقْنَا اجْتِنَابَهْ$$

O Allah, enable me to see the truth as truth and give me the ability to follow it, and enable me to see the falsehood as false and give me the ability to refrain from it.

The ability to see the truth means you can compute, decipher and see things as they are without deluding yourself. With the map, meanings and purpose, we can evaluate whatever we are faced with and awaken in this life to the glory of the presence of Allah.

$$وَهُوَ مَعَكُمْ أَيْنَ مَا كُنْتُمْ$$

And He is with you wherever you may be (57:4)

Imam Ali said, 'There are people who know: find them and learn from them. Then there are people who know, but they do not announce it: so remind them that they know. Then, there are people who don't know: flee from them. And there are people who don't know, but want to know: have sympathy for them.'

We are now living with a category that did not exist in the above description by Imam Ali, i.e. the people who don't know but think they know. These are the most dangerous of people: go very far away from them.

The Prophet Muhammad was one of those who knew, even though he was called *ummi* meaning 'not formally taught'. According to many references, the Prophet Muhammad could read but was not formally trained. Even though he was not tutored formally in reading and writing, people accused him of reading and imitating the original teachings of other scriptures (the Old Testament, Torah, Injeel, etc.). However, if he could read that which is unseen, it stands to reason that he was a special being. His receiving of *wahy* (revelation) indicates that the ultimate truth was revealed to him. *Umm* (mother or original) is the root of the words *ummah* and *ummī*. The Qur'an is called *Umm al-Kitāb*. Allah says, 'I will wipe out many things, but what remains is *Umm al-Kitāb.*'

Our hearts need no formal teaching or tutoring to be selfless. First, you must be aware that there is both a *rūh* (soul) and Allah's presence in you. Then you understand the meaning of the great verse:

$$وَلَا خَوْفٌ عَلَيْهِمْ وَلَا هُمْ يَحْزَنُونَ$$

And no fear will there be concerning them, nor will they grieve.
(2:274)

The origin of the word *khawf* is to fear—the fear of missing out. That you miss the awakening, the opportunity to awaken before it's too late. The *mū'min* (believer) is certain that Allah is with him:

$$لَا تَحْزَنْ إِنَّ ٱللَّهَ مَعَنَا$$

Do not grieve, indeed Allah is with us. (9:40)

Do not be content with or stop at mere outward explanations of the Qur'an. As the Qur'an repeats phrases, so too should you repeat and find reflective explanations. Read recommended commentaries and give yourself time to reflect upon what you have understood. Dive in with conscientiousness and encompass yourself with the knowledge of the Qur'an.

5.2 The Perfect Freedom of No Choice

The entire Qur'an is based on the concept of *akhirah,* what comes later—the infinite and boundless for which the self yearns. We all love to have endless space and freedom. Outer freedom is sought to choose inner freedom ultimately. When we see aspects of life as being efficient, perfect or correct, we respond to the perfection already in existence.

Allah makes it easy for us:

فَٱقْرَءُوا۟ مَا تَيَسَّرَ مِنَ ٱلْقُرْءَانِ

Recite what is easy (for you) from the Qur'an. (73:20)

Read the easy part or what you can and connect with it. Allah wants ease and flow.

In a *Hadith Qudsi*, Allah says: 'My servant does not draw near to Me with anything I love more than what I have made obligatory on him. And My servant continues to draw near to Me with supererogatory actions until I love him. When I love him, I become his hearing with which he hears, his seeing with which he sees, his tongue when he speaks, his hand with which he strikes, and his foot with which he walks. If he were to ask Me for something, I would give it to him. If he were to ask Me for refuge, I would give him refuge.' Sometimes, the *nafilah* (optional act of worship), the *tarawih* (prayer in *Ramadan*) or the additional *salāh* (prayer) are wonderful because you are in that mode. Increase in these actions to rise against your *nafs* (ego). If you are strong enough but sometimes your heart is not attuned, do it anyway to break the *nafs*. The *nafs* is like a wild horse. Break it. Read! *Iqra!* You must read whatever your inner state is according to your level of consciousness. If your consciousness is illumined, then you read in multi-layers.

When our actions begin with, and are under *Bismillah* (in the name of Allah), it is no longer by force because

we see the perfection of layer upon layer of how
Allah has enabled the perfection of existence. Allah
says:

$$\text{قُل لَّوۡ كَانَ ٱلۡبَحۡرُ مِدَادٗا لِّكَلِمَٰتِ رَبِّي لَنَفِدَ ٱلۡبَحۡرُ قَبۡلَ}$$
$$\text{أَن تَنفَدَ كَلِمَٰتُ رَبِّي وَلَوۡ جِئۡنَا بِمِثۡلِهِۦ مَدَدٗا ۝}$$

*Say: If the sea were for (writing) the words of my Lord, the sea
would be exhausted before the words of my Lord were exhausted,
even if We brought the like of it as a supplement. (18:109)*

Every instant, every split second is a *kalimah*. And *kalimah* means many other things, including 'command',
'an impulse', 'an order' or a *'wahy'*, or 'descent'. It
is anything that is a command of Allah, and the
moment is Allah's command. *Qalam* implies what is
written at that moment and what by decree manifests.
Every moment is a combination of many factors
of energies, of entities that have come together at
that instant.

People on their way to being awakened desire only
what is being brought to them. So there is no conflict
between them and what they receive from the world
as a message. Allah is the One Creator of space
and time. Thus, read and contemplate what you

are reading, knowing that the message is timeless and self-empowering

5.3 Calibration

Some of the themes raised in the Qur'an unveil the future. Accordingly, this *dunyā* (world) is a small sample of what comes after death. In questioning the self's readiness for that terrain, the Qur'an presents many maps, descriptions and prescriptions for human needs.

One of the prescriptions is the annual exercise of abstention and restriction, *Ramadan* (month of fasting), which encourages awareness upon awareness. Intelligent seekers of Truth have practised fasting even prior to the time of the Prophet Ibrahim.

Conscious restriction causes the seeker to enter the realm beyond worldly consciousness into a consciousness that goes higher into the Essence and Source of creation. Through this awakened restriction and and restraint from outer immersion in actions and transactions, our journey towards the highest *anwār* (lights) commences. New insight can be gained into the meaning of the purpose, the beginning and the end of existence.

Taking the Qur'an in its entirety, it is a most beautiful, complex, multi-dimensional book of signs, metaphors, instructions, revelations and unveilings. Some verses are very broad. The Qur'an calls man to ponder the rise and fall of prior extinct civilisations that may have been far superior to us. While some verses are very focused. For example, it addresses man:

$$\text{وَأَسِرُّواْ قَوْلَكُمْ أَوِ اجْهَرُواْ بِهِ إِنَّهُ عَلِيمٌ بِذَاتِ الصُّدُورِ ﴿١٣﴾}$$

And conceal your speech or proclaim it. He knows what is in the breasts. (67:13)

Honesty requires courage and for that you need to be present and accountable. Every human being has a divine spirit which is eternal and always reflects truth and its accompanying shadow which is the self/ego.

To truly be kind and just to yourself—read, recite, listen, resonate, and then calibrate.

6. ONENESS AND BALANCE

6.1 Singularity—*Tawhid*

Tawhid (Oneness/Singularity) emerges as soon as we realise that all else (you, I, the world as we experience and know it) originates from the One.

Three hundred odd verses concentrate on *Tawhid*. Oftentimes, where the names of Allah appear, you either find a description of *Tawhid*, requiring the seeker of the One to dissociate anything else with Allah, or *tashbih* (affirming singularity in opposition to declaring incompatibility). For example, 'Allah is the Light of the heavens and the earth' (24:35) is *tashbih*. Equally, Allah reminds us in Chapter 22 (*Hajj*):

مَا قَدَرُواْ ٱللَّهَ حَقَّ قَدْرِهِۦٓ إِنَّ ٱللَّهَ لَقَوِىٌّ عَزِيزٌ ۝

They measure not Allah His rightful measure. Lo! Allah is Strong, Almighty. (22:74)

You and I cannot measure that which is immeasurable. Thus, do not let yourself try to measure as *Allahu Akbar* (Allah is Greater). Submission to the One Source of greatness is all you, as a seeker, can do. That submission is called *Islam*.

Tawhid (Oneness/Singularity) is an unveiling from the essence of the Source and is our singular human ability to know, understand, love and trust the One Sustainer, Creator and Source of all. Allah says:

إِنَّمَا هُوَ إِلَهٌ وَاحِدٌ

Confess, There is only One God, One Creator. (6:19)

Then it says in *Ayat al-Kursi* (the verse of the Throne), which is another description of this fantastic essence of Oneness.

ٱللَّهُ لَآ إِلَهَ إِلَّا هُوَ ٱلْحَيُّ ٱلْقَيُّومُ لَا تَأْخُذُهُ سِنَةٌ وَلَا نَوْمٌ

Allah, none is worthy of worship except He, the Ever-Living and One who Sustains and protects all that exists. Neither slumber nor sleep overtakes Him. (2:255)

We have a lifetime to contemplate the first words of this verse *Allahu la ilaha illa hu* (Allah, none is worthy of worship except He). Our higher self must thus awaken to the *Tawhid* (Oneness/Singularity) of the Source from which all life emanates. Your declaration of verses like 2:255 above and 112:1

below must direct your understanding of the one Truth that there is only One.

$$\text{قُلْ هُوَ ٱللَّهُ أَحَدٌ ۝}$$

Say Allah is One. (112:1)

Through *Tawhid* you begin to understand the conundrum of *wama qadr* (they measure not) from the earlier verse (22:74). You cannot measure the boundaries of Absolute Reality. Only the manifestation of that Light or Reality is never removed from you. It is by grace that you gain insight, yet you will never be able to understand it entirely.

$$\text{وَهُوَ مَعَكُمْ أَيْنَ مَا كُنتُمْ}$$

And He is with you wherever you may be. (57:4)

The traces of *anwar* (lights) will be the only manifestation after all on this earth has disappeared.

$$\text{وَلَا تَدْعُ مَعَ ٱللَّهِ إِلَـٰهًا ءَاخَرَ لَآ إِلَـٰهَ إِلَّا هُوَ كُلُّ شَىْءٍ}$$
$$\text{هَالِكٌ إِلَّا وَجْهَهُ لَهُ ٱلْحُكْمُ وَإِلَيْهِ تُرْجَعُونَ ۝}$$

And call not, besides Allah, on another god. There is no god but He. Everything (that exists) will perish except His own Face. To Him belongs the command, and to Him will ye (all) be brought back. (28:88)

The path of *Tawhid* is confirmed and clarified by great beings like the Prophet Ibrahim. Through the toughest of trials, Prophet Ibrahim had to return to the One constantly. Every one of us has emanated from the One. If we don't refer to the One beyond all, we will invariably make mistakes in our journey through life. The most important thing is Oneness, and the Qur'an warns us against *shirk* (assigning partners to God).

Allah can forgive or cover up anything you and I do as mistakes, except not seeing the One because that is not a mistake but a structural fault.

إِنَّ ٱللَّهَ لَا يَغْفِرُ أَن يُشْرَكَ بِهِۦ وَيَغْفِرُ مَا دُونَ ذَٰلِكَ لِمَن يَشَآءُ وَمَن يُشْرِكْ بِٱللَّهِ فَقَدْ ضَلَّ ضَلَٰلًا بَعِيدًا ﴿١١٦﴾

God forgives not (the sin of) joining other gods with Him; but He forgives whom He pleases other sins than this; one who joins other gods with God has strayed far, far away (from Truth). (4:116)

قُل يَٰعِبَادِىَ ٱلَّذِينَ أَسْرَفُوا عَلَىٰ أَنفُسِهِمْ لَا تَقْنَطُوا مِن رَّحْمَةِ ٱللَّهِ إِنَّ ٱللَّهَ يَغْفِرُ ٱلذُّنُوبَ جَمِيعًا إِنَّهُ هُوَ ٱلْغَفُورُ ٱلرَّحِيمُ ﴿٥٣﴾

Say: O my servants who have transgressed against themselves, do not despair of the mercy of Allah; surely Allah forgives sins altogether; He is indeed the All-Forgiving, the All-Compassionate. (39:53)

We must remedy it. That is why when a mistake, a problem or an issue hits us, we immediately have to say:

$$ لَّآ إِلَٰهَ إِلَّآ أَنتَ سُبْحَٰنَكَ إِنِّى كُنتُ مِنَ ٱلظَّٰلِمِينَ $$

There is no deity except You; exalted are You. Indeed, I have been of the wrongdoers. (21:87)

And refer back to the Doer:

$$ إِنَّا لِلَّهِ وَإِنَّآ إِلَيْهِ رَٰجِعُونَ $$

Indeed, we belong to Allah, and indeed to Him we will return. (2:156)

6.2 Duality

The variety of complementary opposites is infinite; thus, the Qur'an reveals the second most crucial issue: duality. Duality is an understanding and acknowledgement required by the seeker of the endless varieties of dualities or pluralities that surround us, for example, good and bad, day and night, he and she, success and failure, black and white, appropriate and inappropriate, knowledge and ignorance, all of which emanate from the One.

Thus, from the One emanates this amazing creative act of the universe coming into its being and awareness of itself. The cell begins to be aware that it has life. It has sentience, then it grows into its evolutionary cycle through millions of years, ending up with an animal. The animal is aware that it has to feed itself, it goes wherever it can, to sustain itself. Allah says all of these creatures are in a state of glorification.

تُسَبِّحُ لَهُ ٱلسَّمَٰوَٰتُ ٱلسَّبْعُ وَٱلْأَرْضُ وَمَن فِيهِنَّ وَإِن مِّن شَىْءٍ إِلَّا يُسَبِّحُ بِحَمْدِهِ وَلَٰكِن لَّا تَفْقَهُونَ تَسْبِيحَهُمْ إِنَّهُۥ كَانَ حَلِيمًا غَفُورًا ۝

The seven heavens and the earth and all that is therein, glorify Him and there is not a thing but glorifies His Praise. But you understand not their glorification. Truly, He is Ever-Forbearing, Oft-Forgiving. (17:44)

No sustenance is required for the One that is self-sustaining. You and I need to be sustained by air, water, food, etc. That is how we are drawn to be in passionate love with He, Who is self-sufficient and not subject to space and time, whereas every form of life is framed in space and time. Allah declares here:

يَـٰٓأَيُّهَا ٱلنَّاسُ ٱتَّقُواْ رَبَّكُمُ ٱلَّذِى خَلَقَكُم مِّن نَّفْسٍ وَٰحِدَةٍ وَخَلَقَ مِنْهَا زَوْجَهَا وَبَثَّ مِنْهُمَا رِجَالًا كَثِيرًا وَنِسَآءً وَٱتَّقُواْ ٱللَّهَ ٱلَّذِى تَسَآءَلُونَ بِهِۦ وَٱلْأَرْحَامَ إِنَّ ٱللَّهَ كَانَ عَلَيْكُمْ رَقِيبًا ۝

O mankind, fear your Lord, who created you from one soul and created from it its mate and dispersed from both of them many men and women. And fear Allah, through whom you ask one another, and the wombs. Indeed, Allah is ever, over you, an Observer. (4:1)

Man was created from one *rūh* (soul) and its complementary pair was made from it. We should not deny our need for each other, for man and woman, family, neighbourhood, society and community. We cannot grow without social connectivity, social responsibility and dependence on others.

وَمِن كُلِّ شَيْءٍ خَلَقْنَا زَوْجَيْنِ لَعَلَّكُمْ تَذَكَّرُونَ ۞

And of all things We created two mates; perhaps you will remember. (51:49)

There are two of everything. And from these, pairs emanate multiple varieties.

يَٰٓأَيُّهَا ٱلنَّاسُ إِنَّا خَلَقْنَٰكُم مِّن ذَكَرٍ وَأُنثَىٰ وَجَعَلْنَٰكُمْ شُعُوبًا وَقَبَآئِلَ لِتَعَارَفُوٓا۟ إِنَّ أَكْرَمَكُمْ عِندَ ٱللَّهِ أَتْقَىٰكُمْ إِنَّ ٱللَّهَ عَلِيمٌ خَبِيرٌ ۞

O mankind, indeed We have created you from male and female and made you peoples and tribes that you may know one another. Indeed, the most noble of you in the sight of Allah is the most righteous of you. Indeed, Allah is Knowing and Acquainted. (49:13)

You have been created as nations and people of different cultures, languages, and races to meet and find those outward differences. If you are living in a hot country, it's different from when you are living among the Eskimos. While our habits and lifestyles differ, our essential needs are the same. We want contentment, tranquillity, peace, love, well-being and happiness. We want security, we do not want insecurity, and we do not want to be afraid. We cannot go beyond our mind and thoroughly do our *'ibādah'* (worship) if we constantly fear for our life.

The Prophet Muhammad reminds us that the Qur'an says:

إِنَّمَا ٱلْمُؤْمِنُونَ إِخْوَةٌ

Verily, the believers are like brothers. (49:10)

However, only those who have trust and are certain in faith that Allah will guide them will further come to know that original light reflected in their heart. The Prophet also says, *'Look into the mirror of your brother,'* meaning when we see each other, we know we are all the same. We want to act appropriately. Continue this approach to receive continuous guidance regarding what is appropriate for you.

Know that every verse is a verse for you. From each verse will be derived that which its reader needs. This points towards the pure awareness and remembrance which is referred to in the Qur'an by the word *dhikr* (remembrance).

6.3 Balancing Heaven and Earth

The Qur'an reminds us:

قُل مَتَٰعُ ٱلدُّنْيَا قَلِيلٌ وَٱلْأَخِرَةُ خَيْرٌ لِّمَنِ ٱتَّقَىٰ وَلَا تُظْلَمُونَ فَتِيلًا

Say, the enjoyment of this world is little, and the Hereafter is better for he who fears Allah. And injustice will not be done to you even as much as a thread. (4:77)

No matter how much you will get in this world, whether it is wealth, power, status, or influence, it is limited. Yet, what we truly seek is the limitless. Thus, fools continue to strive for their commercial success until they collapse. Politicians only remain in politics until they are disgraced. You and I are 'in' this world, and to not be 'of' this world, which is limited. We have within us a *rūh* (soul) and a light that is pushing us, driving us towards the limitless—Allah.

The Qur'an repeatedly tells us to refer back to Allah. No human being is exempt from age, physical ability and limitations in mental acuity. That is why the Prophet Muhammad always loved people who had *'ifāf* and *kifāf*—i.e. those who gave thanks and were content with what they had. As your higher self takes hold, your point of reference will change from discovering the outer purpose to finding the real purpose of life. The outer purpose is that we all need to survive, but what about the need to arrive? Your approach to the Qur'an should guide you to survive the outer to arrive at the inner. Failing this, your susceptibility to the outer will result in the world engulfing you. The business of living in this world is to achieve a balance between humanity and Divinity. You must not deny the challenges that come with your humanity. Instead, continuously refer to that which is lasting:

$$وَٱلْأَخِرَةُ خَيْرٌ وَأَبْقَىٰ ۝$$

While the Hereafter is better and more enduring. (87:17)

If you are a Muslim, you start believing in the *Akhi-rah* (ultimate realm/what comes after death), which eventually becomes a reality and allows you to see it in front of you. As your approach to the Qur'an takes hold, you are aware of every breath and do not have to be constantly reminded of death. You are alert and aware that the air that goes in at any instant may not come out. Call upon Allah's *Rahmah* (Mercy). You know you are only here to journey towards the next phase. Our *dīn* (religion, life transaction between Allah and man) is founded upon knowing about the next stage, not just believing in and talking about it. You must know that you have been created for it, and the Qur'an is your ultimate navigation tool, with the Abrahamic traditions and *Sunnah* (customary practice, line of conduct used in reference to Allah or the prophet Mohammad) as your guides.

The completion of this journey, according to the Qur'an, is as the Prophet Muhammad says, 'Be in this world with your body and your mind, but be in the *Akhirah* with your heart.' Our desire is for long-term sustainable happiness. The reality is that we often experience five minutes of goodness and ten years of misery.

Allah reminds us that:

$$وَبِٱلْأَخِرَةِ هُمْ يُوقِنُونَ$$

Of the Hereafter they are certain [in faith] (2:4)

The Prophet Muhammad also repeatedly reminds us about *Akhirah* (Hereafter), the abode of eternity. Your deep dive into the essences and fragrances of the Qur'an will reveal the endlessness of the *Akhirah*. *Akhirah* is timeless, where you and I are no longer aware of space and time. The mind goes into another zone as you do in deep sleep. In your approach to the Qur'an, always ensure you keep awareness of the Oneness and duality.

CONCLUSION

Our Prophet Muhammad has commanded us to hold firmly to the Book in later times when the human race will be more divisive. The Book cannot be contradicted. It is evident. It is undistorted, its wonders are never exhausted, and it is ever-fresh and relevant to its reciter. What is intelligence but longing to know the vastness beyond our apparent existence?

To gain a contemporary understanding of the Sacred Book, seeing it as appropriate for all time, we are advised to approach the Qur'an with the realisation that we may leave this world at any minute. Only when the study of the Qur'an has prepared us to depart with joy and good cheer will it bring meaning and application to our desires and supplications.